THE QUILTMAKER'S ART

Contemporary Quilts And Their Makers

Lark Books
50 College Street
Asheville, North Carolina 28801

Cover: *Bittersweet XIV* by Nancy Crow
68½ by 68½ inches
1981

First Edition
ISBN NO. 0-937274-04-6 Library of Congress Catalog Card No.: 82-82472

Copyright © 1982 by Lark Books, a division of Lark Communications Corp.

Published in 1982 by Lark Communications
50 College Street Asheville, North Carolina 28801

TABLE OF CONTENTS

(over)

DEDICATION

To Harriet Powers, 19th century quiltmaker whose name,
likeness and work have survived the passage of time,
and to all those who slipped away before we knew
they were gone . . .

HARRIET POWERS

Harriet Powers. Photo courtesy of Museum of Fine Arts, Boston.

Harriet Powers (1837-1911) was a black farm woman from Athens, Georgia. A former slave, she left a legacy of appliqued quilts that reflected her experience as a Christian woman with an African heritage. Two quilts still in existence depict scenes from the Old and New Testaments mingled with local legends and Powers's own experiences; their imagery and applique construction exhibit a stylistic affinity to West African wall cloths.

A religious woman, Powers committed Biblical passages to memory and drew from them in the designing of her quilts. *Creation of the Animals* (better known as *Bible Quilt*), shown here, is composed of 15 squares with silhouette images containing scenes from Biblical events, including Adam and Eve in the Garden (panel 4), Jonah being swallowed by the whale (panel 6), two animals of each species (panels 7, 9, 14) and the Crucifixion (panel 15).

Although Powers and her husband were land-owning farmers, they hit hard times at the end of the century and she was forced to sell the first of her quilts (now in the collection of the Smithsonian Institution). Jennie Smith, a white schoolteacher who had long admired Powers's work, purchased it for five dollars. She recorded the 1891 sale, saying of Powers:

She arrived one afternoon in front of my door in an ox-cart with the precious burden in her lap encased in a clean flour sack . . . After giving me a full description of each scene with great earnestness, she departed but has been back several times to visit the darling offspring of her brain.

She was only in a measure consoled for its loss when I promised to save her all my scraps.

Smith exhibited the quilt at the Cotton States Exposition in Atlanta in 1895 (in a building constructed with funds raised by the black community to show the agricultural, trade, mechanical and creative activities of participating blacks). As a result of the exposure, Powers received a commission for a second narrative quilt, *Creation of the Animals*. This quilt passed from owner to son to collector to museum; in 1964 it became part of the collection of the Museum of Fine Arts, Boston.

Harriet Powers. The Creation of the Animals
(better known as Bible Quilt), ca. 1895-
1898; pieced and appliqued cotton with
details embroidered in cotton and metallic
yarns, 69 by 105 inches. M. and M. Karolik
Collection, 64.619. Courtesy of Museum of
Fine Arts, Boston.

Tafi Brown. Rocking-
ham Raising: Mortise
and Beetle, *1979;*
cyanotype, machine-
pieced, hand quilted
by E. M. Sweet, 58½
by 61 inches. Photo:
Robert Gere.

INTRODUCTION

Like jazz, the patchwork quilt is an indigenous American art form. And like its musical counterpart, the quilt is a cacophony of colorful, textural, often disparate elements arranged into a rhythmic, vibrant composition.

The history of the American quilt is by now well-known. Its roots go deep into other cultures but the flowering of its expression has taken place here. Waste-not-want-not Colonial women pieced together the fabric scraps of everyday life into a visually charged fabric that served as the top of a three-layer textile sandwich. Filled with cotton or wool and backed with plain cloth, the quilt provided warmth and comfort for cold nights and hard beds.

Usually geometric, boldly colored and arrestingly modern, quilts from their inception are among the finest examples of abstract design, with images drawn from the environment, the home, architecture, history and the entire realm of imagination and experience. That they had a function in no way diminishes their visual impact or the authenticity of their expression.

Quiltmaking was an integral part of a woman's workday, along with the cooking and cleaning, laundry, mending, child caring, wood chopping and gardening. To have made one hand stitched quilt in a lifetime—typically, hundreds of thousands of stitches went into the making of even a coarse utility quilt—is a marvel. To have made one for every member of the family, and have made additional quilts of silk or other fine fabrics for special occasions, is a miracle indeed.

Despite its intensity of concentration and time, quiltmaking was a welcome relief from the sun-up-to-sun-down cycle of domestic chores. In a time when creative options for a woman were as confined and confining as her domestic sphere, quilt-making provided her with an opportunity to express joy, ambition, sorrow and even political sentiment: a visual language created by the mind and hands from snippets of cloth.

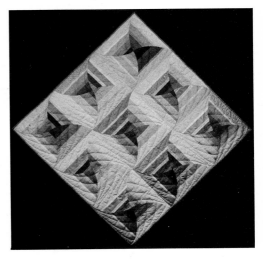

Michael James.
Graded Polychrome
Stripe No. 4, *1982;
machine-pieced
cotton, hand quilted,
polyester batting, 42
by 42 inches.*

Left, Nancy Erickson. Angst, 1980; dyed, stitched, velvet, cotton and satin, 40 by 81 inches. Collection of Bill Boehner. Photo: Jon Schulman.

Below, Radka Donnell. Welcome, 1982; pieced by Radka Donnell, machine-quilted by Claire Mielke, 93 by 71 inches. Photo: Tresch and Wenger.

In the quilting bee that often followed the creation of a quilt top—when other quilters joined to help stitch or tie the pieced top to its other two layers—women had the opportunity to meet and discuss issues of importance to them. Surely it is no coincidence that the first wave of feminism took hold in 19th century America when talk flowed freely while nimble fingers worked a threaded needle in and out of cloth.

Today the lot of women has improved, and the centrally heated 20th century home is substantially warmer than its architectural predecessors, yet the tradition of quilt-making has continued. What is it about the medium of cloth—and the process of cutting up, rearranging and stitching—that draws painters, sculptors, weavers, printmakers and architects to it?

"Laying out and piecing quilts gave me a sense of wholeness and certainty that I had lacked as a painter," says Radka Donnell, whose distinctive abstract works remain functional. Similar expressions are echoed by other artists profiled in *The Quiltmaker's Art*. Says Julie Roach Berner, "In making a quilt I can design, color, cut and assemble pieces to make an integrated whole."

Tactility, with the feelings of warmth and comfort that it engenders, is another fundamental reason for artists having chosen fabric as a creative medium. Nancy Halpern, a former architecture student, says, "Though most of my quilts end up on the wall, I love an excuse to sleep with any one of them. I can combine my love of architecture with this more intimate kind of space." Linda MacDonald finds rewarding "the fusion of disparate elements—cool geometrics with the soft, warm quilt fabric." Michael James puts it most simply: "Nothing else gives me the feeling I experience when I run my hands and eyes over the surface of a quilt."

As it relates to artmaking in general, Joyce Marquess Carey sees quiltmaking as "a little sculptural and a little architectural and a bit like music—building upon a theme bit by bit until the whole form is revealed." Nancy Crow may speak for most

when she says, "Like any art, quiltmaking is a search for that always elusive masterpiece."

The contemporary quiltmaker draws from a rich tradition but is limitlessly free to embellish it with the images, materials and processes of our own time.

Pamela Burg, who works with throwaway materials, finds that "Paper and acetate provide me with an anonymous substance from which my artistic and conceptual expression may grow."

Tafi Brown, an innovator of printed images on cloth, says "The photographic images I use can be traditional or—and this is what I am so intrigued with—they can become abstract images and patterns totally unrelated to the original photograph."

Breaking from the quiltmaking tradition, yet feeling very much a part of it, is often the situation of contemporary artists who work with the materials and processes of quiltmaking while leaving its functional aspect behind. Jody Klein, a maker of wall quilts of printed and stitched paper, has moved into relief paper constructions that she displays in plexiglass boxes. How does this work relate to the quiltmaking? "It is the basic philosophy of quilting—the gathering and assembling of parts—that has been the underlying direction of all my work."

With Klein's words in mind, I began to feel very much like a quiltmaker myself as I worked (with others) on this book. Selecting artists, choosing works, editing statements, I pieced together a fabric of images and words. Indeed, paper and printed images are both used by quiltmakers represented in this volume, and the concept of uniting elements created by various quiltmakers harkens back to the first friendship quilt. Of course this "quilt" can neither be slept under nor displayed on a wall, yet like a stored heirloom quilt that is taken out on special occasions, it need simply be unfolded to warm the spirit and delight the eye.—*Joanne Mattera*

Top, Fraas/Slade. Island, 1981; painted dyes on cotton, machine-quilted, 24 by 24 inches. Photo: Dennis Griggs.

Above, Esther Parkhurst. Four Corners, 1980; machine-pieced, hand quilted, 52 by 52 inches.

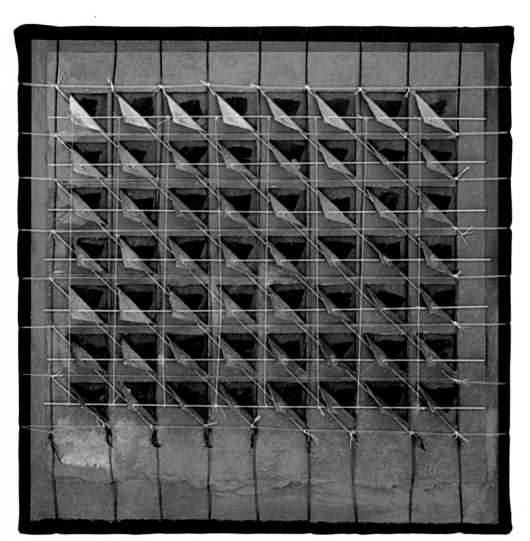

JODY KLEIN

"It is the basic philosophy of quilting—the 'gathering' and the 'assembling' of many parts—that has been the underlying direction of all my work."

Purple Feathers,
1982; mixed media,
12 by 12 by 3 inches.

Jody Klein in her studio. Photo: Martha Swanson

Quiltmaking is a direct development of my printmaking graduate work at Kent State University. For my thesis topic I chose to do a series of prints on cloth rather than on paper. These became my first quilts. In searching for a way to give the flatness of the cloth some dimensionality, I discovered—or rediscovered—quilting. This was in 1965.

My paper quilts of stitched, stamped, painted and colored surfaces are a gathering of the techniques I have used since graduate days. Their cow and motorcycle images are based on my own collection of antique toys and artifacts.

In my most recent "quilts" I have let those images go. I am making assemblage constructions in a grid format of layered paper, painted surfaces, industrial felt, silk organza, metallic threads and silver and wooden rods. All are in 12 by 12 by 3 inch plexiglass boxes. In imposing a size limitation on myself, I am concentrating on the juxtaposition and combinations of opaque, translucent, and iridescent surfaces.

Am I a quilter? I will always feel that I am no matter what I am doing. I save, sort and regroup pieces of fabric, paper and mementoes or artifacts, which I then assemble and organize into a layered, patterned, stitched (or fastened) work that may or may not have a functional use. It is the basic philosophy of quilting—the "gathering" and the "assembling" of many parts—that has been the underlying direction of all my work.

Homunculus Motor-
cycle Riders, *1980;
laminated paper/
fabric, stitched,
printed, 35 by 35
inches.*

RADKA DONNELL

"Laying out and piecing quilts gave me a sense of wholeness and certainty that I had lacked as a painter."

Red Riding Hood's Journey, *1981; 58 by 85 inches.*

Minnie's Love Song,
*1980; 42 by 54
inches.*

Above, Radka Donnell. Right,
Patience, *1982; pieced by the*
artist, machine-quilted by Claire
Mielke, 91 by 61 inches. Photo:
Tresch and Wenger.

In 1965 I broke away from painting and started to make quilts full time. Laying out and piecing the quilts gave me a sense of wholeness and certainty that I had lacked as a painter. In the printed textiles and the piecing process I found a means to express my vital concerns as a woman: my body, my feelings, my relationships to others, my frustrations and my values: tenderness, resourcefulness, endurance.

To get the quilts shown publicly on equal terms with painting became a painful struggle as I insisted that my quilts be viewed as bedcovers *and* appreciated as art—and not be cleansed from their function which, for me, had changed all elements of design into a code for feeling.

Floating, *1982, pieced by Radka Donnell, machine-quilted by Claire Mielke, 88 by 64 inches. Photo: Tresch and Wenger.*

DORLE
STERN-
STRAETER

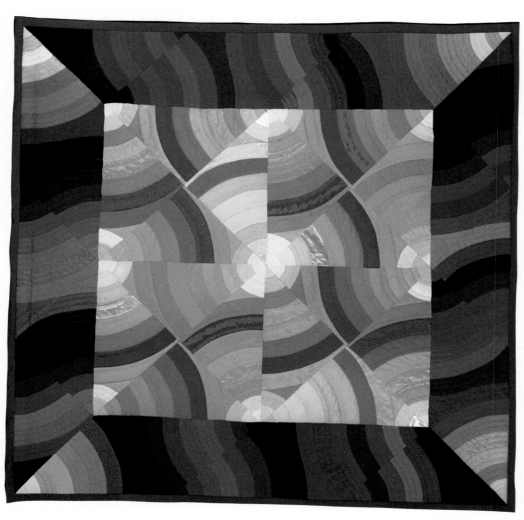

Blues, *1981; 52 by 52 inches. Photo: Ed Fausty.*

20

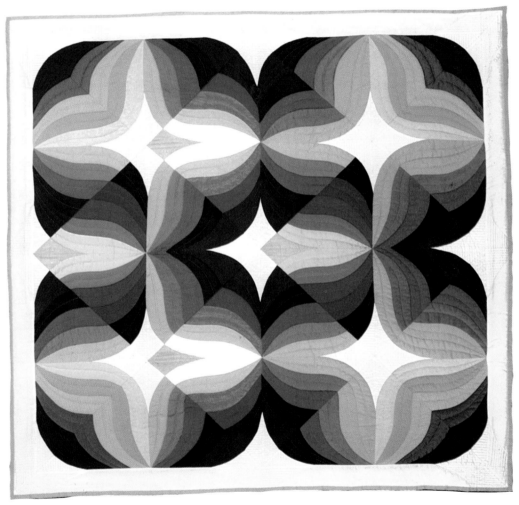

Lotus II, *1981; 51 by 51 inches. Photo: Ed Fausty.*

"I look forward to bringing a traditional American folk art back to Germany as a modern fiber art."

Dorle Stern-Straeter working in her studio, 1981. Photo: Chuck Auerbach.

Ever since I can remember, I have been interested in and have worked with fibers. When I moved to this country with my family from West Germany six years ago, I found my true metier. In our first summer here we visited the Shelburne Museum in Vermont and I knew, seeing all the wonderful quilts there, that I wanted to learn this American folk art.

My first quilts were traditional but after a while I started to make my own contemporary designs. In the last five years I have made over 60 quilts and wall hangings. The forms and structures of the different fabrics fascinate me. I love experimenting with colors and color combinations. It is as if I were painting with the fabric. In breaking away from the traditional quilt, I have also started to use silk, satin, velveteen and chintz in addition to the usual cotton, and I find that I get beautiful effects with these combinations.

I am returning to Germany soon and plan to exhibit, teach and sell my quilts there. I look forward to bringing a traditional American folk art back to my country as a modern fiber art.

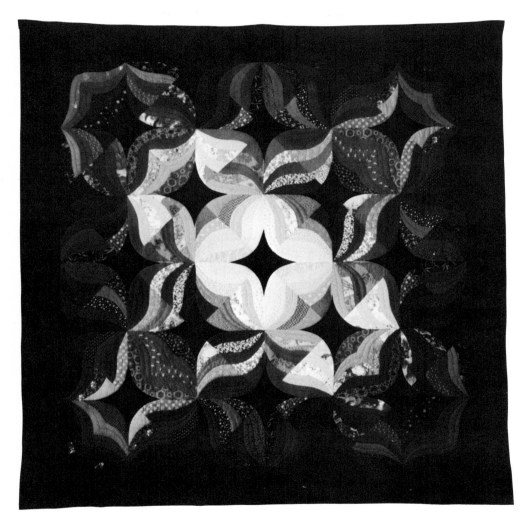

Blue Kaleidoscope,
*1980; 84 by 84
inches. Photo: Ed
Fausty.*

SUSAN SCHROEDER

Series #1 (#6), 1981; batik on cotton, 49½ by 39¼ inches.

24

"I wanted to work in large scale to see if I could handle huge areas of color and pattern."

Series #1 (#8), *1981, batik on cotton, 49½ by 39¼ inches.*

#4, 1980-1981; batik on cotton, 78 by 66½ inches.

In 1970 I began working with quilts and pieced hangings. I had always been interested in textiles (I also weave and sew) and I needed a medium that could be taken up at will as I cared for my baby. I also wanted to work in large scale to see if I could handle huge areas of color and pattern. I had no studio space but lots of floor.

Soon I encountered an old problem: the difficulty in finding just the right color and material that a work demands. To overcome it I began to dye the fabric myself.

In 1980 I was enrolled in the M.F.A. program at Kent State University when all of this came together. I felt at home with batik and liked the accidental halftone effects of dye that seeped under the wax.

I had already experimented with the color possibilities of overdyeing on yarn. The next logical step was to apply those methods to fabric. Using a stock solution dyeing procedure in combination with hot wax resist, I was able to control color and tone with precision. Working with small squares or rectangles of resisted fabric allowed the greatest amount of color exploitation while permitting the entire overdyeing procedure to be revealed in geometric figures. These modules could be pieced together to form a large unified color field.

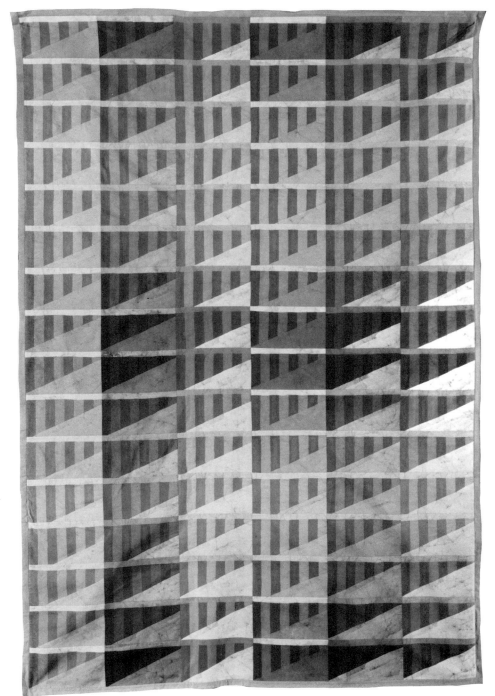

#1, 1980, batik on cotton, 75 by 48½ inches.

27

Series #1 (#5), 1981; batik on cotton, 49¼ by 38½ inches. Photos: Nicholas Hlobeczy

PAMELA JEAN BURG

"My intention is to make a fine art statement that employs a reference to the textile arts and my personal associations with interior architectural spaces."

Terry's Cloth, *1982; paper, 35 by 43 inches.*

Pamela Jean Burg.
Photo: Beatty
MacDonald.

Hood, 1982; paper
construction, 28 by
37 inches. Photo:
Woody Packand.

For whatever reason, I have found myself clinging to the memories of spaces, rooms, buildings, corners and closets which I have lived in, visited, seen or only dreamed about.

Paper and acetate are the materials I have used to create quilts influenced by these memories. Inexpensive and readily available, not high in monetary value, these materials provide me with an anonymous substance from which my artistic and conceptual expression may grow.

The process of sewing to make a fabric is of primary importance to my work. The juxtaposition of materials (acetate and paper) to process (applique and quilting) is essential for creating the suggestion of a quilt. The component parts support each other while also producing a slightly prismatic, quilted plane.

Shroud, *1980; color Xerox on paper, brass screen, thread, hand-woven fabric, ribbon, 9 by 9 by 9 inches.*

Below, Eye-Pick-Nick, *1982; paper, 35 by 43 inches.*

Right, detail of Eye-Pick-Nick.

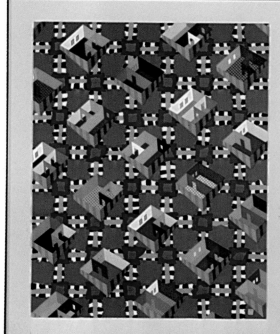

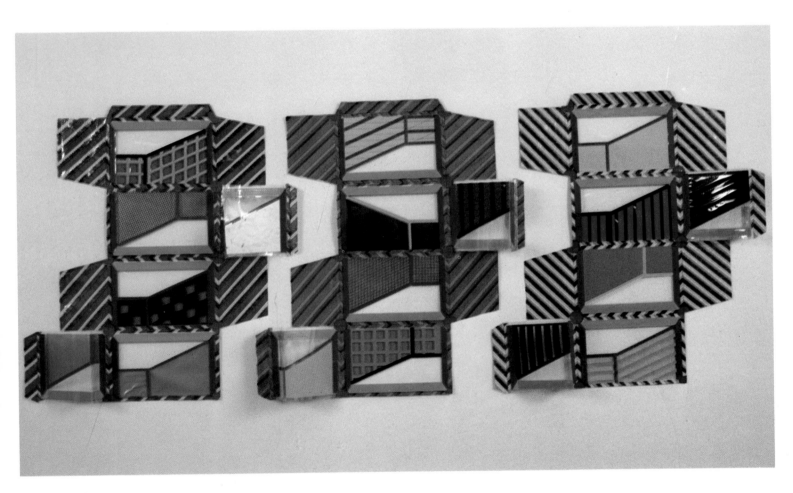

Carton Complex,
1981; color Xerox on
acetate, Mylar, paper,
tape, plastic thread,
30 by 68 by 4 inches.

PAUL WESLEY WALKER

Paul Wesley Walker in his studio, March 1982. Photo: Philip M. McKown.

"After starting to collect old Midwestern quilts, I decided to make one."

As a serious objective painter for over a decade, I became fascinated with the graphic statement of quilts five years ago. My involvement has grown ever since.

The majority of my pieces are hand pieced and hand quilted. I work two hours a night and four hours on weekends and can complete only four or five works annually.

During the past year, I have become involved in dyeing fabric to overcome the color limitations of commercially available material. Procion dyes provide a fantastic range of colors on unbleached muslin. Some recent efforts with Seminole patchwork are giving me a fine, spectral quality that I find exciting.

My themes are relatively varied, from abstract dancers and mandalas to prayer rug motifs and facial profiles. I see no particular limits to the artistic range of quilted textiles and invariably have half a dozen designs as "mental pictures" waiting for the lengthy process each requires. It is only natural, I suppose, that the most important work is the next one.

Arrythmia, *1982; 70 by 76 inches, with preliminary drawing.*

Cosmic Dance, *1981; 49 by 49 inches, with preliminary drawing.*

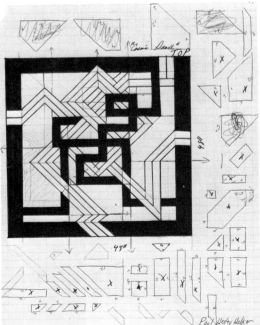

LESLIE FULLER

Iris Quilt, *1981;*
cotton, hand painted
satin, 96 by 106
inches.

"Most of my work is done on a commissioned basis, so quite a bit of effort goes into creating a color scheme and design that relate to the collector's sensitivities and environment."

Leslie Fuller working in her studio, March 1982. Photos: Rick Raphael.

Most of my work is done on a commissioned basis, so quite a bit of effort goes into creating a color scheme and design that relate to the collector's sensitivities and environment. I have designed quilts based on aerial photographs, landscapes and mandalas. One client who is a baseball fan even commissioned a New York Yankees quilt! I am currently working on an Art Deco piece for a New York film producer.

The biggest challenge for me is to balance my client's taste and desires with my own sense of style and design. An essential aspect of this process is my close relationship with the fabric house from which I have bought cloth for many years and which provides me with the wide selection of fabrics necessary to satisfy the tastes of many different collectors.

My quilts are machine-appliqued and hand quilted. I have recently been working with hand painted designs on satin, which I expect will play an increasingly large role in my work. The painting provides a sense of depth and texture that amplifies the appliqued design. I find this effect gives the details an intensity and perspective difficult to achieve with any other technique.

JEAN HEWES

"I draw with my sewing machine."

Flower Girls, *1982;
fabric, 68 by 55
inches.*

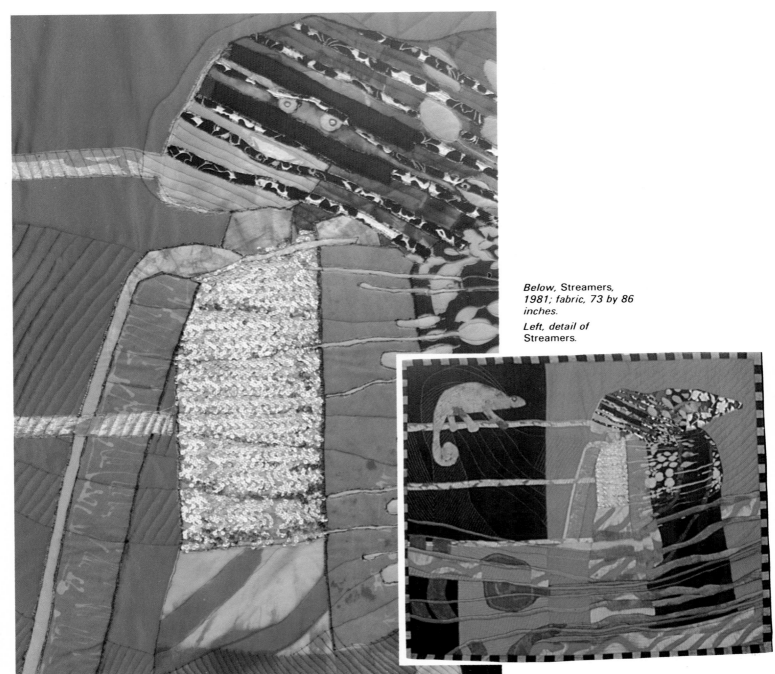

Below, Streamers, *1981; fabric, 73 by 86 inches.*

Left, detail of Streamers.

39

Jean Hewes in front of work in progress. Photo: Robert Hewes.

I started making quilts in 1974 as an escape from the demands of young children. I've always sewn most of my own clothes, so I had access to a large quantity of fabric scraps. I thought of the quilts as fabric puzzles to be used as bedcovers.

My first two quilts were geometric, with an overall format inspired by Persian rugs. I had studied Persian rugs as a design source while my husband and I were Peace Corps volunteers in Iran and spent many spare hours in the Tehran rug bazaar.

My recent work includes figures and glittery fabrics that are remembrances of Iranian tribal women's dresses, some hand quilting of silk and gold threads and lavish borders that act as fabric frames. In these quilts I use a great deal of machine quilted design. I draw with my sewing machine.

I work without a plan or preliminary drawing, finding I achieve a freer, looser look by pinning to the wall a basic background cloth that has been assembled by first throwing various fabrics down on the floor and finding colors, patterns and textures that work well together. Once the beginnings of the quilt are on the wall, I pin additional fabrics to the background as well as pin in a design to be machine stitched.

Beach Birds, *1977;*
fabric, 80 by 111
inches.

41

MICHAEL JAMES

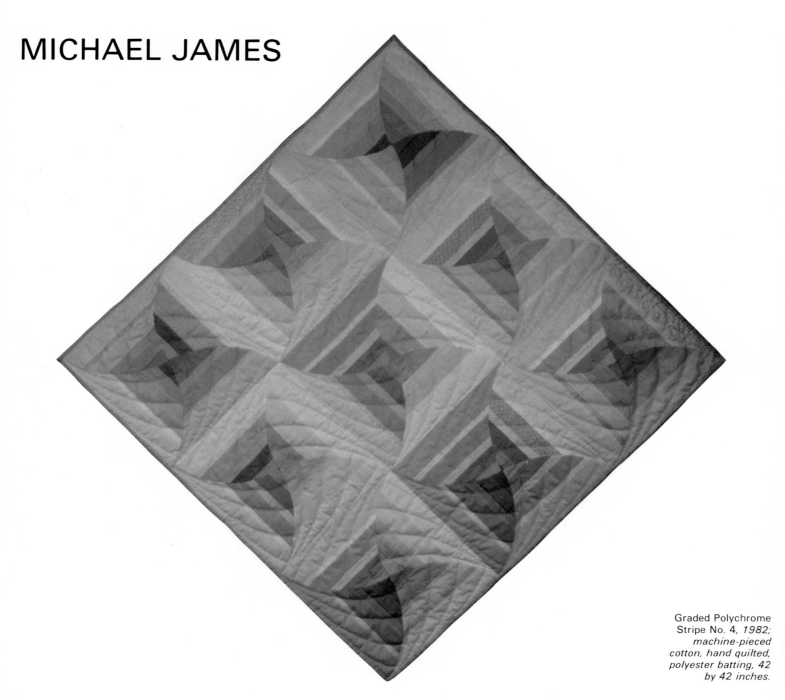

Graded Polychrome
Stripe No. 4, *1982;*
machine-pieced
cotton, hand quilted,
polyester batting, 42
by 42 inches.

Excerpts, *1981; machine-pieced and appliqued cotton, machine and hand quilted, polyester batting, 46 by 70 inches.*

43

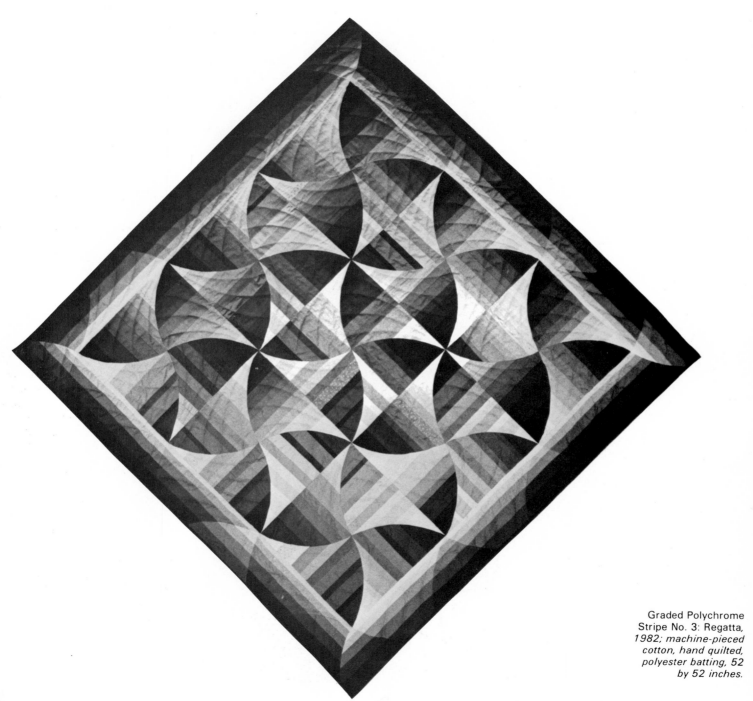

Graded Polychrome
Stripe No. 3: Regatta,
*1982; machine-pieced
cotton, hand quilted,
polyester batting, 52
by 52 inches.*

44

Michael James in his studio. Photos: Judy James.

"I never related to any other medium as well as I relate to fabric, batting and thread."

I'm not too good at offering up weighty explanations for why I do what I do. What first attracted me to quilts, and what has held my attention, is the particular texture of these objects—the result of quilting—that is the exclusive property of these textile sandwiches. Nothing else gives me the feeling I experience when I run my hands and eyes over the surface of a quilt. It's not the history that has kept my attention or the traditional functions associated with quilts; it's simply their physical nature. I never related to any other medium as well as I relate to fabric, batting and thread.

I place no value at all on how long it takes to finish a piece. I place value on how well it is made, on how substantial and relatively successful the image is and on how well these two factors coincide. Up to now I have done all sewing on my quilts myself because my ego prevents me from sharing credit.

45

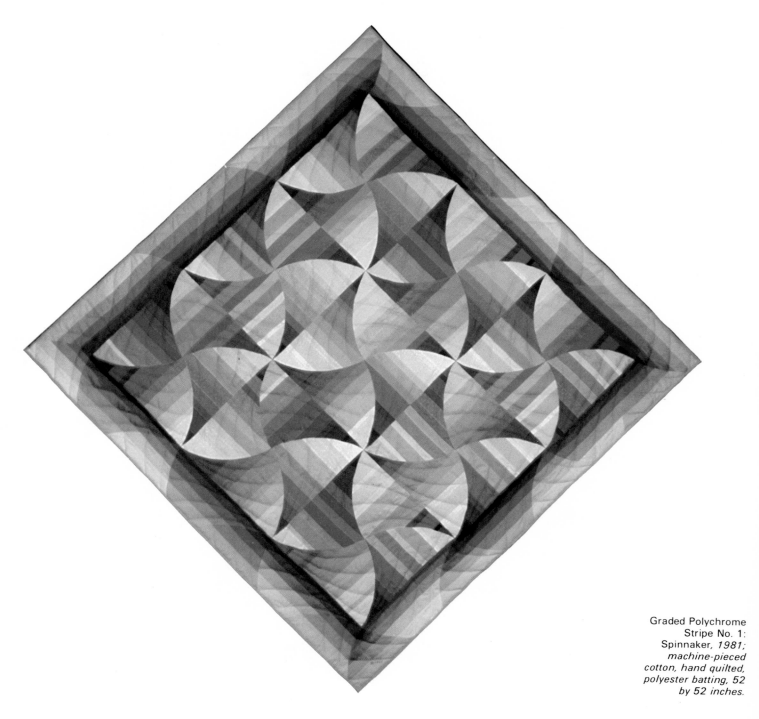

Graded Polychrome
Stripe No. 1:
Spinnaker, *1981;*
machine-pieced
cotton, hand quilted,
polyester batting, 52
by 52 inches.

Stripe Quilt No. 4:
Candylily, *1981;*
machine-pieced
cotton, hand quilted,
polyester batting, 45
by 45 inches.

PATSY ALLEN

*"My favorite
patterning device is
the float."*

Floats, *1981; fabric,
ribbon, 24 by 24
inches.*

In the past few years I have met a number of people who once were weavers. Count me among those people. I studied textiles in college and for several years was a mediocre weaver. As my ideas matured, I realized that weaving was not the discipline for me. I switched to fabric construction. I had been sewing

49

since the age of 15 so my skills were well honed.

The printed patterns of the fabrics in my quilts were a prime concern to me. I also create patterns in the composition. My favorite patterning device is the float. Floats keep reappearing in my work and are strangely reminiscent of the floating yarns of a weaving.

Black Square, *1981; fabric, ribbon, 24 by 24 inches.*

50

JULIE ROACH BERNER

Southwestern Festival, *1980; 78 by 120 inches.*

"In making a quilt, I can design, color, cut and assemble pieces to make an integrated whole."

Above and right, Julie Roach Berner in her studio. Photos: Chris Berner.

I began making quilts during my junior year as a Textiles major at the Kansas City Art Institute. Before that I was making rugs in which the pattern was an integral part of the weaving. I am particularly fond of color and the movement of pattern.

In making a quilt, I can design, color, cut and assemble pieces to make an integrated whole. The great variety of patterns, materials and fabrics available add to the possibilities. I enjoy this multifaceted process and respect the time and skill that goes into the making of a beautiful quilt.

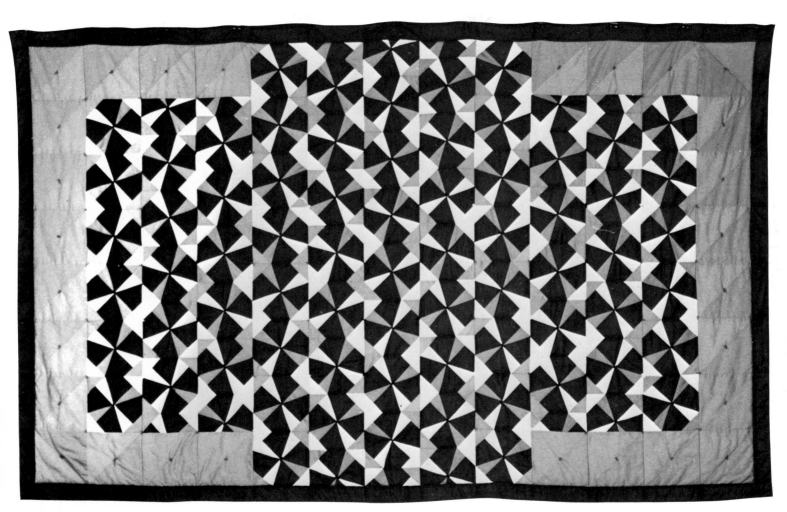

Southwestern
Festival, *1980; 78 by
120 inches.*

DAVID
HORNUNG

The quilt form contains a central paradox: the co-existence of fact (the object) and imagination (the design). Sewing describes the physical limits of the object; stitches insist upon the corporeal. Design, conversely, suggests movement, light and space; it asserts the ethereal. These forces are mutually supportive and enjoy an integrated existence.

I was an abstract painter who worked with constructional processes that evolved into quiltmaking. I prefer to call my pieces "fabric constructions." This term, along with the appearance of my work, clarifies my goals as metaphorical and not functional.

I believe in the future of the non-functional quilted construction. It is plastic enough to project in its specifics the character of contemporary existence while providing a visual experience of durability and richness.

54

"I was an abstract painter who worked with constructional processes that evolved into quiltmaking."

Left, Striped Construction, *1981; 44 by 56 inches. Above,* Calligraphic Construction, *1980; 72 by 72 inches.*

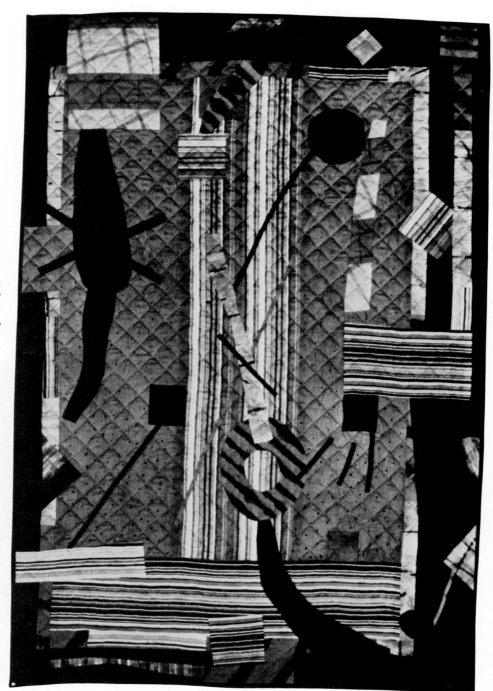

Right, Vertical Con-
struction, *1981; 72 by
48 inches.*

*Below, David
Hornung.*

Blue Construction,
*1980; 60 by 60
inches.*

57

VIRGINIA JACOBS

"The imagery I am involved with is a distillation of the spirit in folk music, dance and costume from around the world."

Right, Cakewalk, 1979; applique, quilted, beaded, 52 by 102 inches.

Below, detail of Cakewalk. Photos: Elliot Kaufman.

Left, the artist with Kolochnik Fantasy. Photo: Rick Echelmayer.

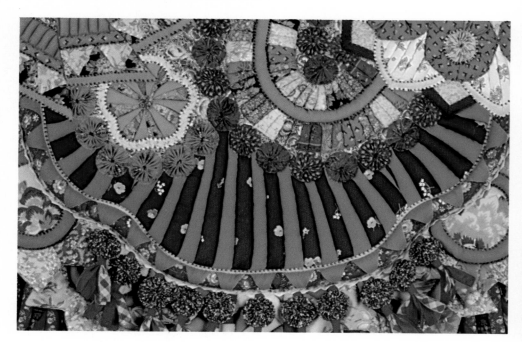

My preference is for forms whose elements don't stop at the edges. I like to encourage anyone working in "quilts" to forego the traditional device of a border and to think of them as more than self-contained compositions within the physical dimensions of the fabric. I want my fabric constructions to imply a continuation and direction into space beyond the limits of the actual material. My background is in architecture and I have learned that a building doesn't end with the last row of bricks or the roof but will always be experienced together with a changing sky, passersby, traffic in the street, the surrounding buildings and the landscape. That sense of context of the world at large is an aspect that I want my fabric constructions to have as part of their existence.

JOYCE MARQUESS CAREY

"I've always enjoyed making things that take a long time."

Joyce Marquess Carey hanging Roy G. Biv.

I've always enjoyed making things that take a long time. Quilting and weaving are contemplative processes, which, once the initial design is worked out, require long comfortable hours of problem solving, construction and finishing. The handwork always gets saved like dessert, to be savored while visiting with friends or listening to music. The stitch, stitch, stitch gives me time to think, to mentally rummage around among unresolved design ideas, to plan; it absolves me from guilt for other work left undone.

I began doing a lot of handwork in the short precious hours when my small children were sleeping, turning uneven bits of time and fabric into something useful. My quilts, like my time, were crazy. Now my life and my work time are more manageable and predictable; my quilts are measured and precise, made of precious impractical fabrics, chosen purely for their aesthetic qualities rather than for their warmth and durability.

I love working with fabrics. They are clean and smell nice. I never tire of the infinite colors and textures nor of the myriad trims, threads and fasteners. It may be the basic modularity of quilting that appeals to me; I start with squared or isometric paper, choose and join the small bits that make up a unit and finally assemble the whole composition. It's a little sculptural and a little architectural and a little bit like music—building upon a theme bit by bit until the whole form is revealed.

Wall Quilt, *1979; 84 by 84 inches.*

61

NANCY CROW

"I love the feel of fabrics. I love sewing with them. I am happiest when I am at work on a piece."

November Study I,
*1980; 64 by 64
inches.*

Bittersweet XIII, *1981;*
95 by 95 inches.
Right, Nancy Crow's
studio.

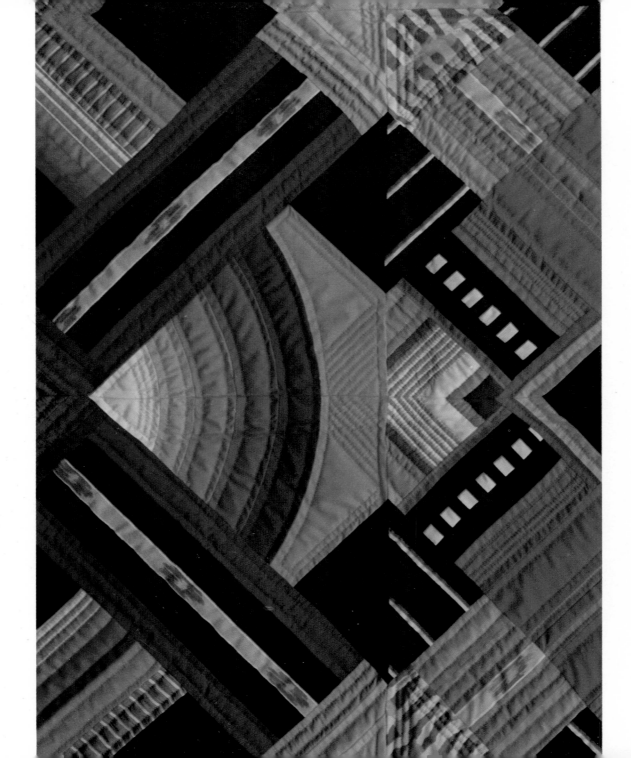

November Study III,
1980; 64 by 64
inches. Detail left.
Right, Nancy Crow.

I have often been asked why I don't paint instead of make quilts, the implication being that quiltmaking cannot be taken seriously. The thought and emotions passing through the brain of a quiltmaker while she works could not possibly be as valid as those of a painter! Such self-righteousness has become boring to me and I find myself impatient with this lack of sensitivity to creation, regardless of medium.

I make quilts mostly because I am driven to. I have no control over the drive. I am happiest when I am at work on a piece. I love the feel of fabrics. I love sewing them. I love using my machine to sew them. I love cutting fabrics. I love trying myriad colors together up on the wall of my studio while seaching intuitively for answers that will fill my soul with excitement and, yes, comfort. The comfort of knowing I am moving in the right direction.

Perhaps I create in homage to my father who taught me to love fine fabrics and who died when I was twelve. He made my sister's winter coat when he was too poor to buy her one.

Like any art, quiltmaking for me is a search for that always elusive masterpiece.

July Study, *1979; 83 by 83 inches.*

Bittersweet XIV,
1981; 68½ by 68½
inches.

FRAAS/SLADE

Gayle Fraas and Duncan W. Slade

Walker Art Museum, 1982; painted Procion dyes on pima cotton, machine-quilted, 25 by 25 inches.

68

"It is in our 'shared vision' that our collaboration grows. This vision stems from our love of pattern and its relationship with architectural elements and landscape vistas."

The Mittens, *1981;
painted Procion dyes
on pima cotton,
machine-quilted, 24
by 24 inches.*

Stairway, *1981; 24 by 24 inches. Right,* Christmas Cove, *1981; 26½ by 26½ inches. Both hand painted, machine-quilted, pima cotton, Procion dyes. Photos: Dennis Griggs.*

71

Right, Gayle Fraas and Duncan W. Slade in their studio.

Below left, Gayle painting stretched fabric for Backfield Swans.

Below right, Duncan working on drawing for Walker Art Museum.

Right, Gayle machine-quilting Walker Art Museum. Duncan ironing fabric for Lizzie Amanda's Quilts. Studio photos: David Isaacson.

Our collaboration began while we were still in school. Satisfying both our needs, we worked on a large quilt, screen printing photo images on the fabric and employing hand and machine quilting. The success of this piece, and the questions it raised, opened the door to the work that followed. Besides screen printing, we pursued batik and other resists, blueprinting, trapunto, applique and sculptural forms, extending into the realm of site-specific and environmental pieces—always exploring fabric as a viable medium to perform our concerns. From the beginning we have used fiber reactive dyes, initially selected because they could be printed leaving the fabric surface unchanged except for the addition of color in an extensive and brilliant range.

Several years ago, disenchanted with the controls that our own technology imposed, we rejected our tools and photo-chemistry for the paintbrush. The dyes yielded to the brush and an ever-expanding number of techniques have developed allowing for subtle wash effects, dry brush and flat, hard-edge solid color areas. Finishing details include machine quilting, which imposes a crisp line to complement beading, and hand stitching, which adds a soft line to the surface.

The direction our work has taken allows each of us to follow our personal concerns. We individually design and execute pieces. It is in our "shared vision" that our collaboration grows. This vision stems from our love of pattern—its design and the magic of its repetition—and its relationship with architectural elements and landscape vistas. It is this blend of surface pattern and illusionary space, which finds roots in both folk and fine arts traditions, that defines and directs our work.

LINDA MACDONALD

New Year's Eve, *1981; cotton, polyester batting, 81 by 92 inches. Photo: Jim Cochran. Left, Linda MacDonald working in her studio. Photo: Bob Comings.*

"I do all my own hand quilting and enjoy it. The stitches add a delicate, ephemeral statement and are another layer of space and illusion to play with as they work within the fabric and color statement."

Neopolitan News,
1982; cotton, poly-
ester batting, 41 by
41 inches. Photo: Jim
Cochran.

The Grange building, a former elementary school, houses Linda MacDonald's studio. Photos: Bob Comings. Opposite page, working drawing for untitled quilt; drawing 13 by 13 inches for quilt 80 inches square.

Over the past ten years I've worked as a graphic artist, calligrapher, map maker and weaver. My involvement with quilts began in 1974. Living in the country in a remote area of Northern California prompted my participation in a weekly women's rap group. Besides our discussion, we wanted to create something tangible and concrete and so we decided to make a quilt; it seemed appropriately rural and woman-oriented, and one of us had already made some crazy quilts.

I had grown up with family quilts from the Midwest made by my great-grandmother and great-aunts so I felt an inherent connection. Yet even though I could weave, crochet, spin, tat and knit, I had never considered approaching quilt-making as a modern medium for art. Unlike other textile mediums it somehow seemed dated and locked in the past.

A turning point came in 1980. I decided to embrace quiltmaking as my art medium and let go of painting and drawing. Early work shows the break-up of the repeated block format and the arrival of planes and layers of space. I'm now interested in exploring the built-in conflicts and tensions inherent in the way quilts are traditionally made. I'm creating dynamically exciting tensions through contradiction. My subject matter is landscapes in geometrics, fields of space moving in counterpoint with lines, small objects and other fields, while being presented in the medium of fabric.

This fusion of disparate elements— cool geometrics with the soft, warm quilt fabric—rewards me. The American quilt is not dated or locked in the past but is the arena of a new frontier.

appliqué

curly black quilting on light

quilting lines light fabric

ft gray

pieced

quilt focus on image

pieced

may try appliqué

appliqué

?

blacks, grays, whites, pastels

ANN TRUSTY

I enjoy working very large, and many of my pieces are stretched tautly over wooden frames. My primary concerns are color, pattern and the relationship of the work with the architectural spaces in which it will be displayed.

I begin my work by rendering a loose watercolor "sketch," my flexible guide for the piece to be created. I cut hundreds of fabric squares and dye them in various shades. I screen print them as many as ten times, and often I hand paint them. I then lay the squares on a table and arrange them carefully. The arrangement changes every day for several days and many squares are discarded. After I have made the final arrangement, I stitch squares together. Surface stitching or painting is added at this point.

My work is a continual struggle of, in my own way, attempting to organize chaos and objectify my emotions into structured patterns and colors. Upon completion, the work surprises me. It has developed its own personality and begins to tell me about myself. I learn from studying it and living with it for a time. Throughout all the changes in life, my art is my one constant.

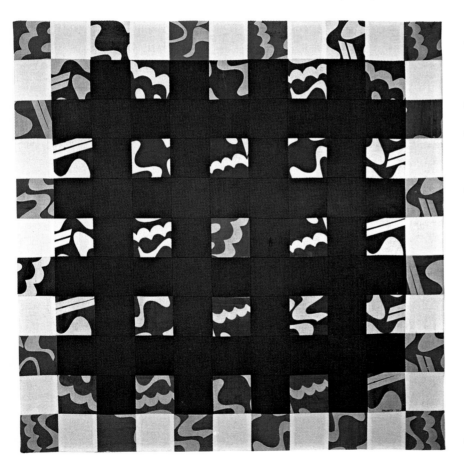

"My background in weaving has contributed to the strong horizontal/vertical patterns in my quilts. I continue to weave, although my concentration is on the sewn work."

Between The Lines, 1981; dyed, screen printed, sewn, 42 by 42 inches.

Left, Ann Trusty with Long Island Sound *draped over loom and* Continuum *on her left. Photo: Joseph Larese.*

Ann Trusty screen printing fabric squares, 1981. Photo: Joseph Larese.

Vertigo, *1981;*
stitched, dyed, screen
printed, sewn. Photo:
William Swan.

JOY SAVILLE

Seminole Study, I,
1981; Seminole
patchwork, reverse
applique, quilted, 39
by 31 inches.

Seminole Study, II:
Tiding, *1981-1982;
Seminole patchwork,
quilted, 79 by 88
inches.*

*"I believe quilting
has always been a
form of
communication.
It provides a
universal language."*

My work is a form of response. A large
part of that response was and is an
intense need to integrate an unex-
pressed part of my self into my daily life.

My focus on exploration with Seminole
patchwork, reverse applique and free
machine-stitchery provides a framework
to say visually what cannot be communi-
cated in other ways. I have chosen these
techniques because of the freedom they
allow, and I enjoy using the sewing
machine as a tool. I can respond intuitively when discoveries are made in

83

pattern, color and form—expressing the rhythms and interrelationships within me.

I rarely draw a design before I begin, preferring instead to abandon preconceptions and remain open to mysteries. Sometimes this means being seduced by the fabric, color, pattern or the design as it is revealed. It involves me completely. (Commissioned work does require a drawing for communication purposes.) I am attracted to abstract geometrical design because of the order resulting out of chaos. Natural forms provide a rhythmical and lyrical quality of expression.

My goals are to continue to challenge my perceptions, to explore and develop untouched aspects of myself and to discover new ways of understanding and expression. Sometimes the questions *What am I doing? What am I trying to say?* are partially answered. At other times they are irrelevant and the process is more than an answer.

Left, Seminole Study, III: Gravity and Grace, *1981-1982; Seminole patchwork, quilted, 92 by 68 inches. Above, Joy Saville. Photos: John Young.*

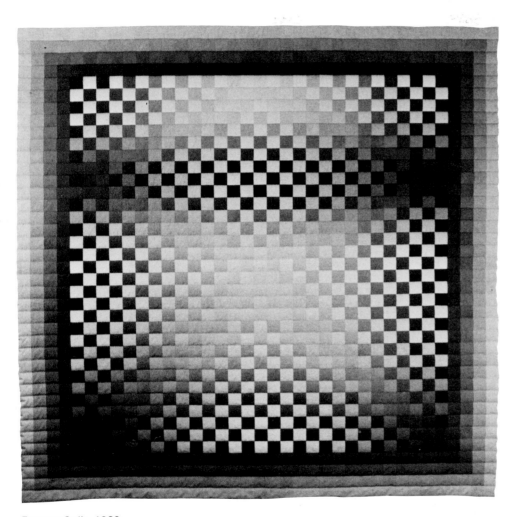

Equator Quilt, *1982;*
dyed cotton, machine-
pieced and quilted, 84
by 80 inches.

JAN MYERS

"I have steered clear
of complicated
piecing and hand
quilting, wanting
instead to develop a
way of working that
maintains the
integrity of the
tradition and *allows*
me to support
myself with my
work."

Remembering
Chicken Little, *1981;*
dyed cotton, machine-
pieced and quilted, 42
by 47 inches.

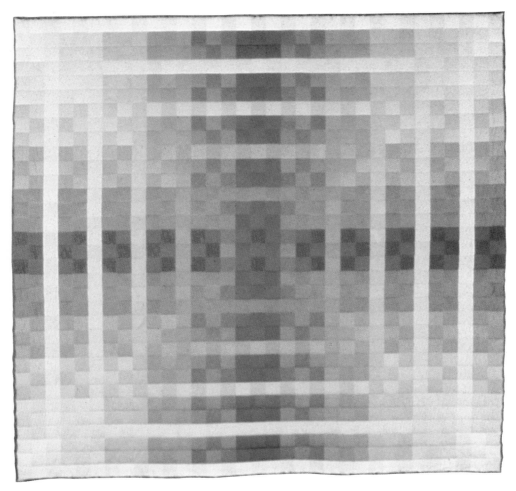

Down The Rabbit
Hole, *1981; dyed
cotton, machine-
pieced and quilted, 82
by 82 inches.*

I came to quilting through the "back door," having never pieced or quilted a traditional block. I did, however, arrive with love and respect for quilts, since I grew up with the work of the women in my family before me.

I came to quilting from a background in art—drawing and printmaking—and began thinking in terms of fabric while doing graduate work in design. Really, the quilts were born out of a curiosity to know whether fabric could present color "tricks" as effectively as paper does. I had to dye the fabric to get the colors I wanted. For design and construction ease I chose the square as my quilt block, and I have been with this format ever since.

The first quilts were tight, orderly and very calculated. But as I work more and more with these expansive color fields, I find that I am free to explore intuitively. The underlying theme remains the same in all of the work: color and light. When designing, I aim for color and value place-ment that will give each work its own light.

I continue to use fabric that I have dyed in gradated sequences (from light to dark, hue to hue) with Procion dyes. I dye yardage, then cut and piece. In general, I have steered clear of complicated piecing and hand quilting, wanting instead to develop a way of working that maintains the integrity of the tradition *and* allows me to support myself with my work.

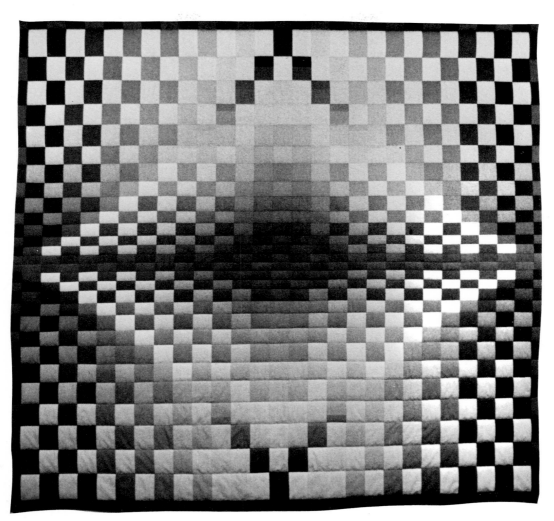

Gem, *1982; dyed cotton, machine-pieced and quilted, 65 by 65 inches.*

CHARLOTTE PATERA

"I have no desire to duplicate old patterns, as much as I love them. I have my own statements to make."

Molistic, 1980; applique, 37 by 39 inches.

Reflections, *1978;*
applique, 70 by 70
inches.

In the early '50s I began working as an artist in the field of package design. The graphic, hard edge way of communicating appealed to me.

In the early '60s I turned to yarns and fabrics for freer expression. I worked with embroidery, needlepoint and especially applique. After working by hand and machine, I found I liked hand work best. I like folk and ethnic art, and have always been excited by the work of the Kuna Indians of the San Blas Islands of Panama.

I started to explore my own techniques of cutwork applique, mixing a few of the Kuna techniques with my own. Quilts provide a wonderful showcase for the applique as well as being functional. I have no desire to duplicate old patterns, as much as I love them. I have my own statements to make which are always searching for ways to be expressed.

I like solid colors. To me, printed fabrics are an interference. They interrupt my images with their images. I like and use certain symbols: birds represent the freedom I seek; flowers, plant life, growth and the need to blossom regularly; butterflies, transformation, beauty and timing; sun, my need to transfer warmth and joy to others.

Above, Charlotte Patera in front of Anamola *wearing a reverse applique apron.*

Right, Mexican Images, *1973; reverse applique, 68 by 73 inches. Photos: Rick Tang.*

Thistle, *1978;
machine-pieced, hand
quilted, cottons and
blends, 96 by 96
inches.*

NANCY HALPERN

*"Somewhere amid
the interplay of
design, fabric and
subject matter, I hope
to create quilts in
which the images
and ideas are free,
floating, moving out
to set off a chain of
new ones in the
observer."*

When I first started making quilts over
ten years ago, I felt I was turning in the
abrasive, sharp-angled world of architecture school for a comforting, privately-
padded cell. For a couple of years I
worked alone, quietly immersing myself
in traditional patterns and techniques.
Then my family and friends gently shoved

me out into my first job, the beginning of an ever-widening and immensely stimulating career involving teaching, writing, traveling and exhibitions. My energy for these activities is always generated by the *making* of the quilts themselves.

At first I intended my quilts to be totally functional, and only through the mistake of making one too "good" for hard use did I come to understand the equally valid function of visually warming a space. Now, though most of my quilts end up on walls, I love an excuse to sleep with any one of them. I've found a way to combine my love of architecture with this more intimate kind of shelter.

My quilts seem more abstract than they used to be, but I think that I'm just dealing with more elusive ideas. Instead of a warm town under snow, I may try to show a dream town I must reluctantly leave at sunrise. Or I try for the translucent quality of light and shadow, sun and fog, through which small islands appear and disappear. My main concerns these days are to avoid the obvious, to tackle rough problems, to find interesting solutions.

Above, Floating World III: (Deer Isle Fog), *1981; machine-pieced, hand quilted, 33 by 43 inches.*

Right, Nancy Halpern. Photo: Isidore Samuels.

94

NANCY GIPPLE

"In designing my quilts, I use strong, frequently unconventional color combinations with shapes that produce high visual energy levels."

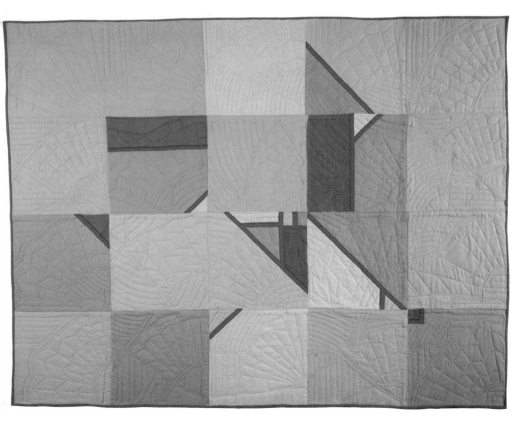

Seashell Fan Club, 1981; bed or wall quilt made of cotton and cotton blend fabrics, 74 by 94 inches.

My fiber pieces are of two distinct types, one sculptural and textural in nature and the other utilitarian.

In my sculptural wall reliefs I have been exploring and interpreting inter-relationships of various shapes, textures and colors in nature. I work with com-binations of materials: textiles, ropes, handspun fiber cables, wood, found objects, plastic and wire.

Then there are my more down-to-earth quilts, non-objective works suitable for hanging or for use as bedding. They are composed of machine washable, dryable, colorfast, commercial fabrics. I prefer these practical, available materials to hand dyed fabrics because of the diffi-culties and health hazards inherent in hand dyeing and because of the durability and ease of care of the final product. In designing my quilts I use strong, frequently unconventional color combinations with shapes that produce high visual energy levels. Almost entirely machine-sewn with all seams double stitched, they are constructed for durability and long service.

The contrast between these two fiber involvements provides me with feelings of freshness and excitement and leads me on into new landscapes and adventures. I believe this is reflected in my products.

ESTHER PARKHURST

"I use assembly line methods of piecing on the machine, but I continue to hand quilt my work because I find that the contrapuntal overlay is an important ingredient of the design."

Floating Circles, 1981; machine-pieced, hand quilted, 54 by 46 inches.

Esther Parkhurst
working in her studio.
Photo: Ken Parkhurst.

I feel that all of my previous experience has prepared me for designing and making wall quilts. During my roles as weaver, seamstress, interior designer, homemaker, mother and color consultant, there always seemed to be something missing. Since mid-1976, quilting has provided me with that elusive element. Perhaps it is recognition or the change to combine both art and craft. Perhaps it is a sense of connection with the past, particularly with the women of the past, or the simple tactile pleasure I feel when working with beautiful fabric. Whatever it is, I love it.

Most of my early pieces were symmetrical and contained central images. Many incorporated the clamshell pattern, a form that still intrigues me. In 1979, I began to make designs with an overall repeat, some of which were asymmetrical, if not in the design itself at least in the random placement of color. In designing, I like to use a basic element such as a triangle, square, hexagon or a quarter circle and develop it until its multiples form a whole. The design possibilities of these forms seem endless. I experience the multiples as reconciling or dealing with the opposites

99

to create something new. Color, to me, is possibly even more important than form; it is the most challenging element of my work, and the most difficult to resolve.

I work with finely woven cotton or cotton and rayon or synthetic mixtures. I use both solid and patterned fabric. Once I've determined the basic design I experiment with it on graph paper, then begin cutting the fabric and putting the pieces in place on my studio wall. The fiberboard wall is covered with white napped cloth so that individually cut shapes of fabric will cling to it and can be pinned as needed.

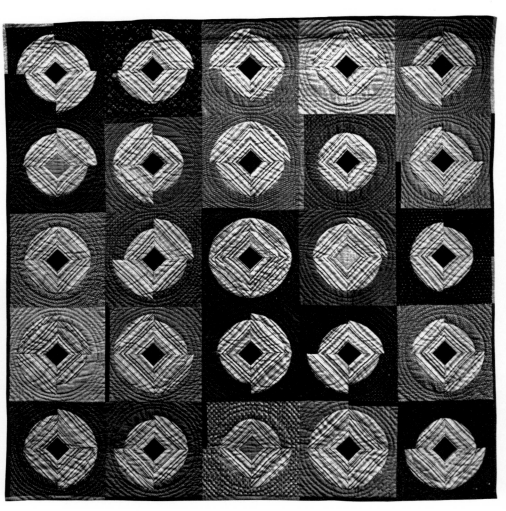

Broken Circles, *1981; machine-pieced, hand quilted, 60 by 60 inches. Detail above.*

NANCY CLEARWATER HERMAN

"I think of the prints as chords and the solid fabrics as notes in a melody."

Gypsy Rondo, *1981; satin and cotton, 58 by 58 inches.*

After The Rain, *1980;
satin and cotton, 36
by 36 inches. Right,
Nancy Clearwater
Herman with* 3 Part
Fugue, *1981. Photo:
Ken Kaufman.*

I am an artist who is primarily interested in color progressions (the way colors change one another as they move from the center to the outside edge of a composition). I work in paint as well as fabric and am at present working with computer graphics.

I use fabric because of the beauty of its texture and the richness of the patterns available. Using a variety of prints in one work is like having the talents of several artists at your disposal for so much a yard. I think of the prints as chords and the solids as notes in a melody, satins as instruments that play light colors beautifully and velvets as instruments rich in low tones.

I model all my work after music because I feel it stands alone as an art form that can move the emotions to great depths without reference to anything but itself.

103

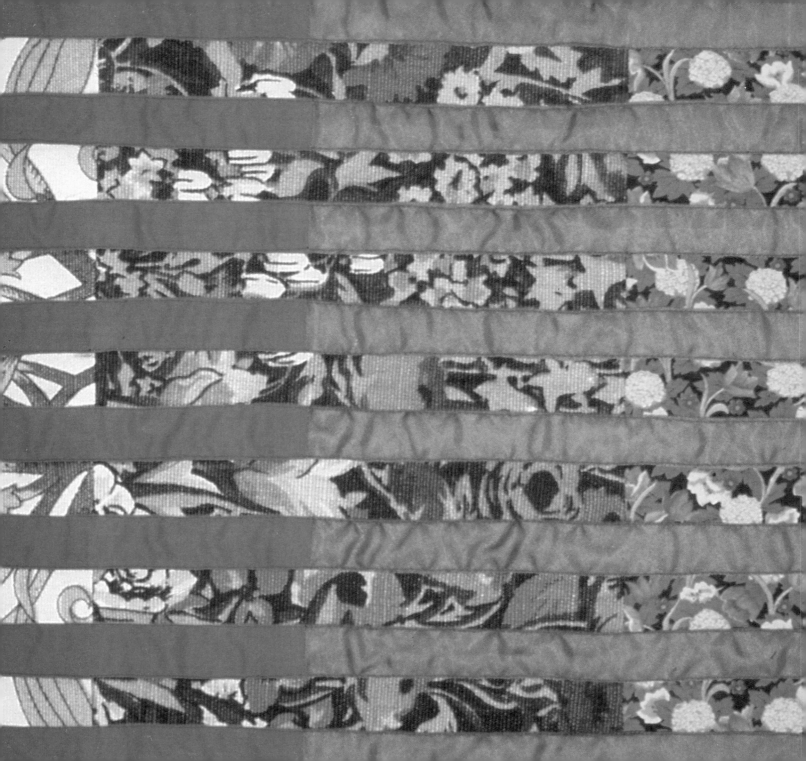

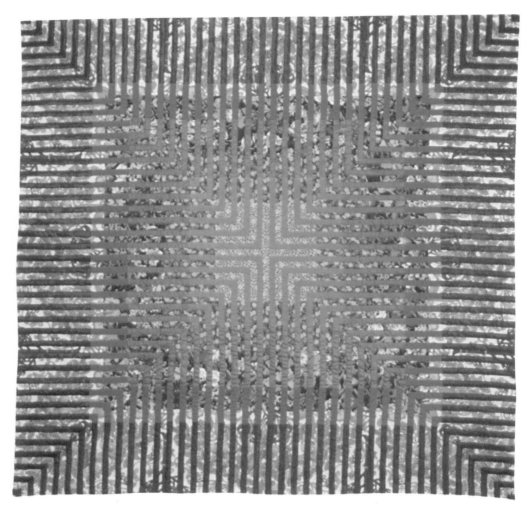

Liberty Garden, 1982;
60 by 60 inches.
Detail left.

WENDA F. VON WEISE

"I use photographs to fabricate landscapes that might be seen in dreams."

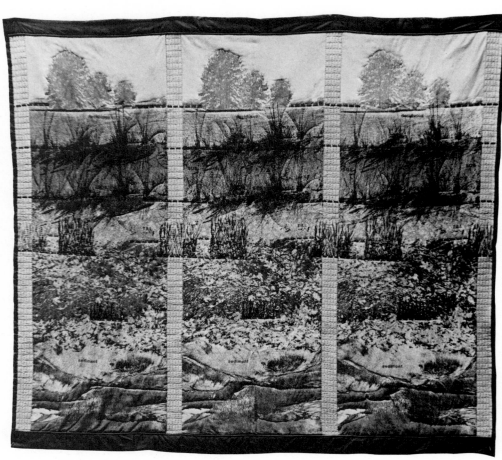

Fabricated Landscape:
Straight Furrows In
Geologic Time, *1979;
photo screen prints
on silk, pieced and
quilted, 73 by 80
inches. Right, Wenda
von Weise with quilts.
Photo: David Wilder.*

I use photographs of the textural elements of water, grass, sand and leaves or of city vistas to fabricate landscapes or cityscapes that might be seen in dreams. My photographs are printed on fabric and then pieced together to create reality as interpreted by the subconscious.

Structurally, the image is used within the context of old pieced quilt patterns, such as the straight furrow or variations of the three, four and nine patch systems.

NANCY ERICKSON

Angst, 1980; dyed,
appliqued fabrics
stretched on a frame,
40 by 81 inches.

"Ideas float above us—I just pull them out and try to mediate them through a sewing machine."

Shadow Cats, *1980;
dyed, appliqued
fabrics stretched on a
frame, 40 by 81
inches.*

Fabric work is so versatile—that is one of its major attractions. It is possible to do large nine by nine-foot fabric paintings, stretch them on a frame if I wish, hang them on walls, over windows (insulation in this cold climate), put them on beds or wear them. Since I work with natural subject matter and prefer large images, most of these "wall warmers" really do look best on a wall, but the multiple-use idea is still attractive to me.

If fabrics were not available, I'd simply be using something else—wood can be carved, charcoal can be drawn with—but right now velvet, satin, muslin, paint and a good sewing machine are perfect. The process is quite direct: I get a general idea, make a small drawing, put swatches of fabrics together on a big wall to work as brush strokes (I have bags of "brush strokes") and work from the feelings fed back from these color relationships. The work is changing right up to the end. I continue to use representational elements reflecting an attachment to the Montana land and an interest in living beings in general. Our rabbit has fascinating, unexpected aspects to her psyche so she appears in my work in various guises, as do snow leopards and other animals.

Left, The Guardians of Fiery Mountain, *1982; velvet, satin and cotton, appliqued, 86 by 49 inches.*

Right, Nancy Erickson in front of Passage Through Fire: Fire Series #1. *Photos: Jon Schulman.*

The Last Dance Of
Fall, *1979-1980; dyed
and painted cotton,
velvet and satin, 108
by 114 inches. Photo:
Jon Schulman.*

Painted Cats, Painted Mountains, *1980; muslin, machine stitched, painted, heat set, 96 by 68 inches.*

KATHLEEN KNIPPEL

My environment and surroundings have been the most important sources for my art. Living in Florence, Italy, has been a fountain of inspiration for me. Everything I see—on my way to classes, at museums, while shopping or just looking—fills me with thoughts and ideas. I am in love with this city and desire to make a personal and impressive statement about it.

I have been doing soft sculpture batik pieces since 1970. Here in Florence the wonderful relief sculptures in bronze and marble have inspired me to try a similar form in fabric.

Above, Kathleen Knippel
working on My Kitchen And
Garden. *Left,* My Kitchen And
Garden, *1982; batik, applique,
quilting on cotton, 26 by 26
inches. Far left, Kathleen
Knippel in garden that inspired
the work.*

"My environment and surroundings
have been the most important sources
for my art."

JANET KOIKE

"It is an honor to make a quilt."

*NYC/Beach, 1982;
silk-screen and resist-
painted dye on silk,
tied, 99½ by 95½
inches. Detail at left.*

The process of quiltmaking is a strange one. When I make a quilt, I'm a housewife without the kids and husband. I wash the fabric, dry it, dye it, iron it and sew it. Designing is intellectual and passionate, but doing the piece requires a love of tedium. Those hours are filled with thoughts, daydreams, cycles of emotions. Good feelings turn into sadness, and frustrated boredom turns into a meditative calm. When I've finished, there it is: my vision realized. Time has passed, something has been learned.

I spend hours studying traditional American quilts and classical Japanese designs, but I also look at Eva Hesse,

117

swimming pools and pictures in magazines. Then I chuck them all. Each quilt is a painting for me, but a quilt also has a function. In the present-day world of mass-produced things, a unique, finely crafted object becomes a statement of the quality of life I believe in. It really is an honor to make a quilt.

Above, Janet Koike in her studio. Right, Bedroom Window, 1980; silk-screen and resist-painted dye on silk, tied, 81 by 90 inches.

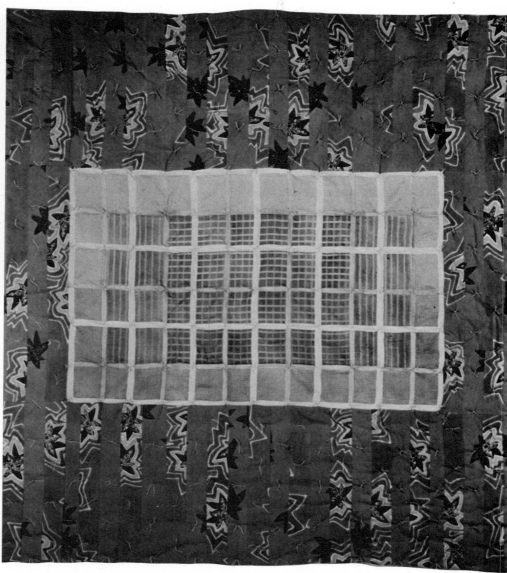

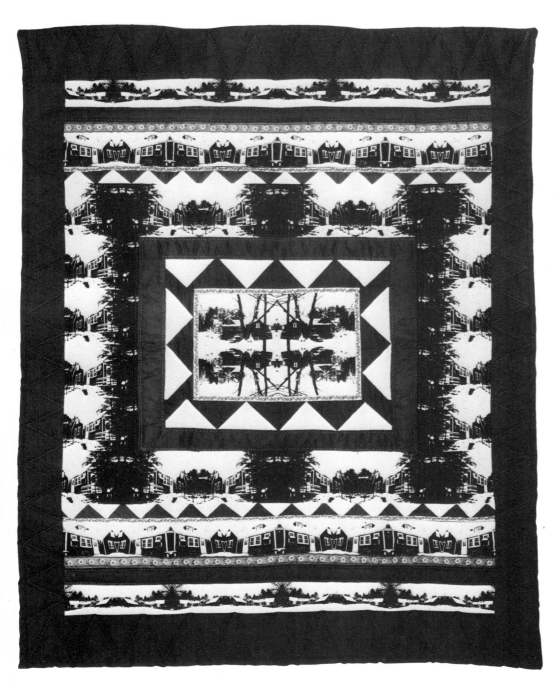

TAFI BROWN

"I make quilts about things that are important in my life at a given time."

The Bley's Place,
1981; cyanotype,
machine-pieced and
embroidered, hand
quilted by M. Bragg,
40½ by 51 inches.
Photo: Robert Gere.

119

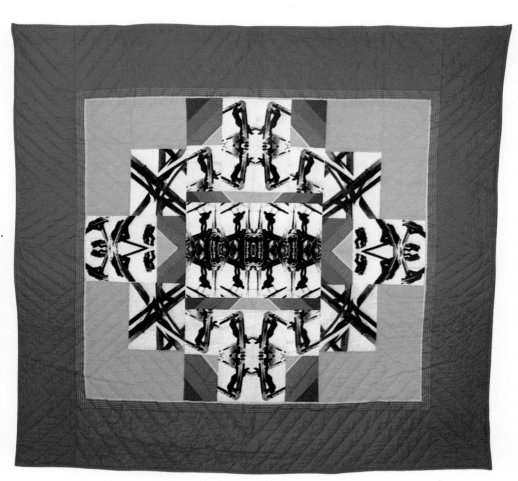

Rockingham Raising: Mortise and Beetle; cyanotype, quilted by E. M. Sweet, 58 by 61 inches. Photo: Robert Gere.

Our lifestyles and our art influence each other and as artists we have to be aware of and take advantage of that. Therefore, I was not surprised in the mid-1970s to find myself turning from ceramics to fabric as my means of expression. I had attended a conference sponsored by the Northeast region of the American Crafts Council to learn how to put photographs on ceramics. Serendipitously I wandered into a workshop on cyanotypes.

I thought the instructor was nuts to be putting a blueprint on fabric; I knew it would fade in a few months because we were in the process of building our own house and the working blueprints disappeared. But when she said that the cyanotype is archival—it's the original blueprint process developed by Sir John Herschel in the 1840s—I began to get interested because I had been documenting the construction of our house with many slides. Why not make an heirloom quilt about our house-building? I made

Right, Tafi Brown in a rare moment: doing her own quilting and using a pair of forceps to pull the needle through. Photo: Robert H. Brown.

the quilt. It was a very personal documentation of one family's building its home. But, down in one corner I happened to have flip-flopped some negatives and I noticed a very interesting pattern. That small corner was the beginning of a new form of expression for me: the cyanotype pieced quilt.

Iconographically I have found the cyanotype process to be quite fascinating: I make quilts about things that are, and for people who are, important in my life at a given time. I make quilts for people of the things they love. These quilts can be used on beds or they can be hung on a wall. The images can be straightforward and traditional or—and this is what I am so intrigued with—they can become abstract images and patterns, totally unrelated to the original photograph. This multiplicity of meanings and uses is so important and so fascinating to me that I must keep making these quilts for people.

Rockingham Raising:
The Sling, *1980;
cyanotype, machine-
pieced, hand quilted
by E. M. Sweet, 65½
by 94½ inches.
Collection of The
Georgia Power
Corporation. Photo:
Finney. Detail at right.
Photo: Robert Gere.*

The American Wing
IX, *1977; cotton,
polyester, polyester
batting, cyanotype
prints, machine-
pieced, hand quilted
by E. M. Sweet, 60 by
90 inches. Collection
of I.B.M., Essex
Junction, Vermont.
Photo: Michael
Gordon.*

INDEX/BIOGRAPHIES

ing: *A Renaissance*, a Midwest traveling exhibition, and a one-woman show at the Missoula Museum of the Arts in 1981.

68-73 **FRAAS/SLADE**
Box 232, River Road
North Edgecomb, ME 04556

Gayle Fraas and Duncan Slade met while students at Southern Connecticut State College in New Haven, Connecticut, in the early '70s. They went on to exhibit—recent work has been shown at the Hand and the Spirit Gallery in Scottsdale, Arizona, 1981, and Gallery on the Green, Lexington, Massachusetts, 1982—and to work as artists-in-residence, recently at Artpark in Lewiston, New York, and at Adrian College, Adrian, Michigan.

36-37 **LESLIE FULLER**
R.D. 1
Sandgate, VT 05250

Leslie Fuller is a self-taught quiltmaker who divides her time between her Vermont home and a New York City studio. Her work has been shown from Boston to California and featured in *House Beautiful, Fiberarts, The Fiberarts Design Book* (Lark) and *The Contemporary Quilt* (Dutton). In addition to executing quilts on a commission basis, Fuller works as an illustrator and a makeup artist for motion pictures.

95-97 **NANCY GIPPLE**
24 Duck Pass Road
White Bear Lake, MN 55110

Nancy Gipple has exhibited her quilts through the Midwest, most recently at

Quilt National '81 in Athens, Ohio. Since 1978 she has operated a fiber studio in St. Paul. Her work can be seen in *The New American Quilt* (Lark).

93-94 **NANCY HALPERN**

Nancy Halpern studied at Radcliffe College, the University of California at Berkeley and the Boston Architectural Center before turning to quilting, which she taught herself to do. She has exhibited her work throughout New England and is represented in two traveling exhibitions: *New Directions: Clay and Fiber* (originating at Eastern Carolina University, Greenville, N.C.) and *Art in Craft: The Haystack Tradition* (originating at Bowdoin College, Brunswick, Maine).

Her work has been included in such periodicals as *Quilters Newsletter, Fiberarts* and *Country Journal* and in several important books: *Quiltmakers' Handbook I and II* (Prentice-Hall) and *The New American Quilt* (Lark).

101-105 **NANCY CLEARWATER HERMAN**
275 N. Latches Lane
Merion, PA 19066

Nancy Clearwater Herman's studies in color and design have involved her not only in quilting but in music and computer graphics. Recent exhibitions of her work have included the *Marietta College Crafts National* in Marietta, Ohio, 1981, and the *Northeast Craft Fair at Rhinebeck*, New York, 1980 and 1981. Her work has been shown in *Fiberarts*.

38-41 **JEAN HEWES**
15075 Garden Hill Drive
Los Gatos, CA 95030

Jean Hewes comes to quiltmaking with

a background in art (B.A. 1965, Lawrence University, Appleton, Wisconsin) and ceramics (M.F.A. 1966, University of Wisconsin, Madison). She has exhibited her recent work at *Innovations in Fiber II* in Denver, Colorado, 1982, and *Quilt National '81*, where she was recognized for the Most Innovative Use of Medium.

54-57 **DAVID HORNUNG**
104 Home Avenue
Providence, RI 02908

David Hornung is a quiltmaker with a background in painting (M.F.A. 1976, University of Wisconsin, Madison). His recent work has been shown at the Rockwell Gallery in Cambridge, Massachusetts, and at *Quilt National '81* in Athens, Ohio, where he received an Award of Excellence. Hornung currently teaches drawing and design at the Rhode Island School of Design in Providence.

58-59 **VIRGINIA JACOBS**
304 South Sixteenth Street
Philadelphia, PA 19102

Virginia Jacobs learned to sew in the 8th grade. After majoring in architecture and receiving a B.A. in 1965 from the University of Pennsylvania, she returned to sewing. Her work has been included in *Quilt National '81*, a 1981 exhibition at Philadelphia College of Textiles and Science and *Needle Expressions '80*, where she received First Prize.

Jacobs lectures frequently about quilting, most recently at the Pacific Fibre Friendship Conference in Hawaii, and has appeared in a segment of

Quilting II, WBGU-TV's series of quilters and quilting in America.

42-47 MICHAEL JAMES
258 Old Colony Avenue
Somerset Village, MA 02726

Michael James is a self-taught quiltmaker with a background in painting and printmaking (B.F.A. 1971, Southeastern Massachusetts University, North Dartmouth; M.F.A. 1973, Rochester Institute of Technology).

James's two publications, *The Quiltmaker's Handbook: A Guide to Design and Construction* and *The Quiltmaker's Handbook: Creative Approaches to Contemporary Quilt Design*, were published by Prentice-Hall in 1978 and 1981 and have been reprinted several times since. In addition to exhibiting and writing, James lectures frequently throughout the United States.

13-15 JODY KLEIN
Waltham, MA

Jody Klein's printed paper quilts were conceived after training in painting and printmaking (B.S. Painting, M.A. Printmaking, Kent State University). Her works have been shown widely throughout the United States, including *The Object as Poet* in 1976, *The Animal Image: Contemporary Objects and the Beast* in 1981 and the *Renwick Souvenir Exhibition* in 1982, all at the Renwick Museum in Washington, D.C.; a one-woman exhibition, *Visual Paradigms*, at the Betsy Van Buren Gallery in Cambridge, Massachusetts, 1981, and *Art in Craft: The Haystack Tradition*, a New England touring exhibition.

Her work has been shown in *Fiberarts* magazine and in *The Contemporary Quilt* (Dutton).

114-115 KATHLEEN KNIPPLE
Via Guelfa 69
Florence, Italy 50122

Kathleen Knipple specialized in textile design while at California State University in Los Angeles (B.A. 1965, M.A. 1967). Although teaching full time since then, she has exhibited extensively, both in California and in Florence, Italy, where she now lives.

Knipple's work has been included in *The Fiberarts Design Book* (Lark), and in Dona Meilach's *Soft Sculpture* and *Batik and Tie Dye* (Crown).

116-117 JANET KOIKE
11411 Center Street
Oakland, CA 94607

Janet Koike has trained extensively for degrees in painting, sculpture, ceramics and textiles at the University of the Pacific, Stockton, California; California College of Arts and Crafts, Oakland; Penland School of Crafts, Penland, North Carolina; and Fiberworks and Pacific Basin Textiles, both in Berkeley, California. Her influences range from potter Shoji Hamada to painter Sonia Delaunay.

Her business, Koike Textiles, specializes in commissioned textiles for interior decorators and clothing designers.

74-77 LINDA MACDONALD
Studio #6, 291 School Street
Willits, CA 95490

Linda MacDonald is a self-taught quilter with a background in art (B.A., San Francisco State University). Recent exhibitions include the *Marin Quilt and Needlework Show*, where she was awarded First Prize in 1980 and 1981, *Quilt National '81* and *Stitchery '81* in Pittsburgh, Pennsylvania.

Her work has been included in *The New American Quilt* (Lark) and *Quilting, Patchwork and Applique* (Sunset).

60-61 JOYCE MARQUESS CAREY
913 Harrison Street
Madison, WI 53711

Joyce Marquess Carey has exhibited her quilts in numerous group shows, including *Innovations in Fiber II*, sponsored by Skyloom Fibers in Denver, Colorado, 1982; *Contemporary Quilting: A Renaissance*, a Midwest traveling exhibition, and *Quilt National '79*. *Fiberarts* and *Interweave* magazines have featured her work, which has also appeared in *The Contemporary Quilt* (Dutton) and *The Fiberarts Design Book* (Lark).

Marquess Carey is an assistant professor at the University of Wisconsin-Madison, where she teaches weaving and stitchery.

85-89 JAN MYERS
4232 Longfellow Avenue
Minneapolis, MN 55407

Jan Myers is a self-taught quiltmaker with a varied educational background. She holds a B.A. in Religion and Asian Studies (1972) and an M.A. in Design, which she received from the University of Minnesota, St. Paul (1979).

Her quilts have been included in several recent exhibitions: *Great New Quilts*, St. Louis, Missouri, 1982; *American Traditions: Contemporary Interpretation*, Sign of the Swan Gallery, Philadelphia, 1982; *Minnesota Women 81*, The Women's Art Registry of Minnesota in Minneapolis and *Quilt National '81*.

Among the publications in which Myers's work has appeared are *Fiberarts*, *American Craft* and *The New American Quilt* (Lark). Myers lectures frequently and has executed private and corporate commissions.

98-100 ESTHER PARKHURST
6677 Drexel Avenue
Los Angeles, CA

Although she has no formal art training, Esther Parkhurst learned to sew as a child and works intuitively, feeling that she has absorbed a great deal as a result of exposure to good design from a 36 year marriage to a graphic design consultant and friends in related fields.

Her public commissions include quilts for the corporate offices of Columbia Pictures in Burbank, California; Hyatt-Regency Hotel lobby, Ft. Worth, Texas, and the Chicago O'Hare Hilton Hotel. Her work has been shown in *Fiberarts, Quilter's Newsletter* and *Fortune* magazines and in *The New American Quilt* and *The Fiberarts Design Book* (Lark).

90-92 CHARLOTTE PATERA
15 Sequoia Glen Lane
Novato, CA 94947

Charlotte Patera is a self-taught artist who has spent 30 years as a full-time, free-lance package designer. Her mola-style quilts have been shown throughout California, including the *Santa Rosa Quilt Show*, where she received Second Prize in 1978.

Fiberarts has featured her work. *Family Circle, Woman's Day, Good Housekeeping* and *Ladies Home Journal* have featured her quilt projects. Patera is the author of *The Mola Pattern Book*, self-published in 1979.

82-84 JOY W. SAVILLE

Joy W. Saville is a self-taught quilter whose most recent work has been exhibited in a one-woman show at the Squibb Galleries, Princeton, New Jersey, 1982, and in such group exhibitions as *Fiber: New Dimensions*, the Gayle Willson Gallery, Southampton, New York; *Quilt National '81* and *Needle Expressions*, 1980, sponsored by the National Standards Council of American Embroiderers in St. Louis, Missouri.

Saville's work can be seen in *The Complete Book of Seminole Patchwork* by Rush and Wittman (Madrona), *the New American Quilt* and *The Fiberarts Design Book* (Lark).

24-28 SUSAN SCHROEDER

Susan Schroeder received a B.S. in education from Kent State University (1962) and is currently enrolled in the M.F.A. program there.

She has exhibited her quilts throughout Ohio, including *Surface Design*, a four-woman show at Hiram College, where she currently teaches, and *Quilt National '81*.

Schroeder is represented in *The New American Quilt* (Lark) and appears in *Quilting II*, a 13-part public television series.

20-23 DORLE STERN-STRAETER

Dorle Stern-Straeter began quilting when she came to the United States from Germany several years ago. She has studied with Michael James and Beth and Jeffrey Gutcheon and has gone on to offer her own workshops in curved seaming.

Recent exhibitions include *Quilt National '81* and a 1982 solo exhibition at the Textile Museum in Heidelberg, West Germany.

78-81 ANN TRUSTY
Lawes Lane, Route 9D
Garrison, New York 10524

Ann Trusty holds a B.F.A. in textile design from the University of Kansas, Lawrence (1976). She has exhibited her work in *Fiber: New Dimensions*, at the Gayle Willson Gallery in Southampton, New York, and *Quilts '82* at the Maple Hill Craft Gallery in Auburn, Maine, both in 1982, and in a one-woman exhibition at the Hemisphere Club at Rockefeller Center in New York City, 1981.

Her work has been reviewed in *Fiberarts*.

106-107 WENDA VON WEISE

Wenda von Weise is a widely exhibited quiltmaker who has specialized in photographic imagery on cloth. She holds an M.F.A. in fiber from Cranbrook Academy of Art (1978), where she studied with Gerhardt Knodel, and a B.F.A. from Cleveland Institute (1975), where she majored in textile design and minored in photography and where she now teaches textile design.

She has been represented in *Fiberarts, Craft Horizons* and *American Craft* magazines and in *The Contemporary Quilt* (Dutton) and *The New American Quilt* (Lark).

34-35 PAUL WESLEY WALKER
Rural Route 3, Box 25
Nashville, IN 47448

Paul Wesley Walker holds a B.A. in fine arts and an M.A. in art education (both from Indiana University, 1975, 1980). An art instructor, he has exhibited his works in *Quilt National '81* and the *Marietta College Crafts National*, 1980, where he received the "Hand and Spirit" award.

His work has been included in *The New American Quilt* (Lark).

BIBLIOGRAPHY

The artists represented in this book have cited the following publications as instructive or inspirational.

BOOKS

Albers, Anni. *On Designing.* Middletown, Conn.: Wesleyan University Press, 1962.

Albers, Josef. *The Interaction of Color.* New Haven, Conn.: Yale University Press, 1963 (revised edition—original limited edition available at some libraries).

Avery, Virginia. *The Big Book of Applique.* New York: Charles Scribner's Sons, 1978.

Bishop, Robert and Elizabeth Safunda. *Gallery of Amish Quilts: Design Diversity from a Plain People.* New York: E.P. Dutton, 1976.

Bishop, Robert. *New Discoveries in American Quilts.* New York: E.P. Dutton, 1975.

Chase, Pattie and Mimi Dolbier. *The Contemporary Quilt: New American Quilts & Fabric Art.* New York: E.P. Dutton, 1978.

Chicago, Judy. *Dinner Party.* New York: Anchor Press div. of Doubleday & Co., Inc., 1979.

Chicago, Judy with Susan Hill. *Embroidering Our Heritage: The Dinner Party Needlework.* New York: Doubleday & Co., Inc., 1980.

Chicago, Judy. *Through the Flower: My Struggle as A Woman Artist.* New York: Doubleday & Co., Inc., 1977.

Christie, Archibald H. *Pattern Design: An Introduction to the Study of Formal Ornament.* New York: Dover Publications, Inc., 1969.

Cohen, Arthur A. *Sonia Delaunay.* New York: Harry N. Abrams, Inc., 1975.

Colby, Averil. *Quilting.* New York: Charles Scribner's Sons, 1979.

Da Conceicao, Maria. *Wearable Art: Innovative Designs for Clothing & Fibers.* New York: Penguin Books, 1980.

Fanning, Robbie and Tony. *The Complete Book of Machine Quilting.* Radnor, Penn.: Chilton Book Company, 1980.

Editors of *Fiberarts* Magazine. *The Fiberarts Design Book.* Asheville, N.C.: Lark Books, 1980.

Finley, Ruth E. *Old Patchwork Quilts.* Watertown, Mass.: Charles L. Branford Company, 1971.

Fisher, Katherine and Elizabeth Kay. *Quilting in Squares.* New York: Charles Scribner's Sons, 1978.

Gutcheon, Beth. *The Perfect Patchwork Primer.* New York: Penguin Books, 1974.

Haders, Phyllis. *Sunshine and Shadow: The Amish and Their Quilts.* New York: Universe Books, 1976.

Henri, Robert. Margery A. Ryerson, ed. *The Art Spirit.* New York: Harper & Row, Inc., 1960.

Holstein, Jonathan. *The Pieced Quilt.* Boston: New York Graphic Society, 1973.

Horwitz, Elinor L. *Contemporary American Folk Artists.* New York: Harper & Row, Inc., 1975.

Houck, Carter and Myron Miller. *American Quilts and How to Make Them.* New York: Charles Scribner's Sons, 1975.

Itten, Johannes. *The Art of Color.* New York: Van Nostrand Reinhold, 1973.

Itten, Johannes. *Design and Form: The Basic Course at the Bauhaus.* New York: Van Nostrand Reinhold, 1975.

Itten, Johannes. *The Elements of Color.* New York: Van Nostrand Reinhold, 1970.

James, Michael. *The Quiltmaker's Handbook.* Englewood Cliffs, N.J.: Prentice-Hall, Inc., 1978.

James, Michael. *The Second Quiltmaker's Handbook.* Englewood Cliffs, N.J.: Prentice-Hall, Inc., 1981.

Johnston, Meda P. and Glen Kaufman. *Design on Fabrics.* New York: Van Nostrand Reinhold, 1981 (2nd ed.).

Justema, William. *The Pleasures of Pattern*. New York: Van Nostrand Reinhold, 1982.

Larsen, Jack L. and Alfred Buhler. *The Dyer's Art*. New York: Van Nostrand Reinhold, 1977.

Laury, Jean Ray. *Quilts and Coverlets*. New York: Van Nostrand Reinhold, 1970.

Lippard, Lucy R. *Eva Hesse*. New York: New York University Press, 1976.

MacDowell, Marsha and Betty MacDowell and Kurt Dewhurst. *Artists in Aprons: Folk Art by American Women*. New York: E.P. Dutton, 1979.

McKendry, Ruth. *Traditional Quilts and Bed Coverings*. New York: Van Nostrand Reinhold, 1980.

Mills, Susan W. *Illustrated Index to Traditional American Quilt Patterns*. New York: Arco Publishing, Inc., 1980.

Morgan, Mary and Dee Mosteller. *Trapunto and Other Forms of Raised Quilting*. New York: Charles Scribner's Sons, 1981.

Needleman, Carla. *The Work of Craft*. New York: Alfred A. Knopf, Inc., 1979.

Pevsner, Nikolaus. *Pioneers of Modern Design*. New York: Penguin Books, 1961.

Porcella, Yvonne. *Pieced Clothing*. Modesto, Calif.: Porcella Studios, 1980.

Porcella, Yvonne. *Pieced Clothing Variations*. Modesto, Calif.: Porcella Studios, 1981.

Proctor, Richard M. *The Principles of Pattern for Craftsmen and Designers*. New York: Van Nostrand Reinhold, 1976.

Risinger, Hettie. *Innovative Machine Quilting*. New York: Sterling Publishing Co., 1980.

Ruddick, Sara and Pamela Daniels, eds. *Working It Out: 23 Women Writers, Artists, Scientists, & Scholars Talk About Their Lives & Work*. New York: Pantheon Books, Inc., 1978.

Rush, Beverly and Lassie Wittman. *Complete Book of Seminole Patchwork: From Traditional Patterns to Contemporary Uses*. Austin, Tex.: Madrona Press, Inc., 1981.

Safford, Carleton L. and Robert Bishop. *America's Quilts and Coverlets*. New York: E.P. Dutton, 1980.

Svennas, Elsie. *Advanced Quilting*. New York: Charles Scribner's Sons, 1980.

Weeks, Linda S. and Jo Ippolito Christensen. *Quilting: Patchwork and Trapunto*. New York: Sterling Publishing Co., Inc., 1980.

Wong, Wucius. *Principles of Two-Dimensional Design*. New York: Van Nostrand Reinhold, 1972.

Woodard, Thomas K. and Blanche Greenstein. *Crib Quilts: And Other Small Wonders*. New York: E.P. Dutton, 1981.

PERIODICALS

American Craft. 401 Park Avenue South, New York, New York 10016.

Artforum. 667 Madison Avenue, New York, New York 10021.

Art in America. 850 Third Avenue, New York, New York 10022.

ARTnews. 122 East 42 Street, New York, New York 10168.

Crafts. 8 Waterloo Place, London, England SW1Y4AT.

Fiberarts. 50 College Street, Asheville, North Carolina 28801.

The Flying Needle. P.O. Box N578, Northfield, Illinois 60093.

Portfolio. 271 Madison Avenue, New York, New York 10016.

Quilter's Newsletter. 6700 West 44 Avenue, Wheatridge, Colorado 80033.

Surface Design Journal. 311 East Washington Street, Fayetteville, Tennessee 37334.

ABOUT THE EDITOR

Joanne Mattera is the editor of *Fiber-arts*, a bimonthly magazine that features contemporary textiles and the artists who make them. A textile artist herself, she has exhibited her work in group and one-woman shows throughout the United States and in Europe, including the 9th International Biennial of Tapestry in Lausanne, Switzerland, in 1979 and the 3rd International Exhibition of Miniature Textiles in Szombatheley, Hungary, in 1980.

Mattera is the author of *Navajo Techniques For Today's Weaver* and *Rugweaving,* both published by Watson-Guptill Publications. This is her first book for Lark Communications.

PRODUCTION STAFF

Layout: *Keiko Yanaga*

Typesetting: *Elaine Thompson*

Keiko Yanaga works as an advertising artist for a retail chain in Asheville, North Carolina and does free-lance work for Lark Communications. Elaine Thompson, a Lark regular, typesets *Fiberarts* and *Handmade.*